ADULT COLORING BOOK
Copyright © 2016 James Linc

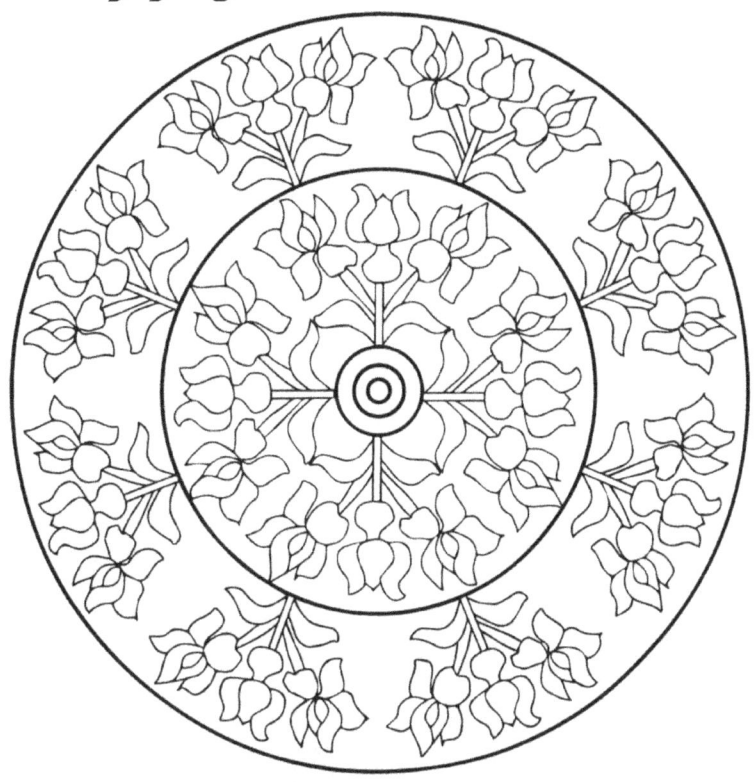

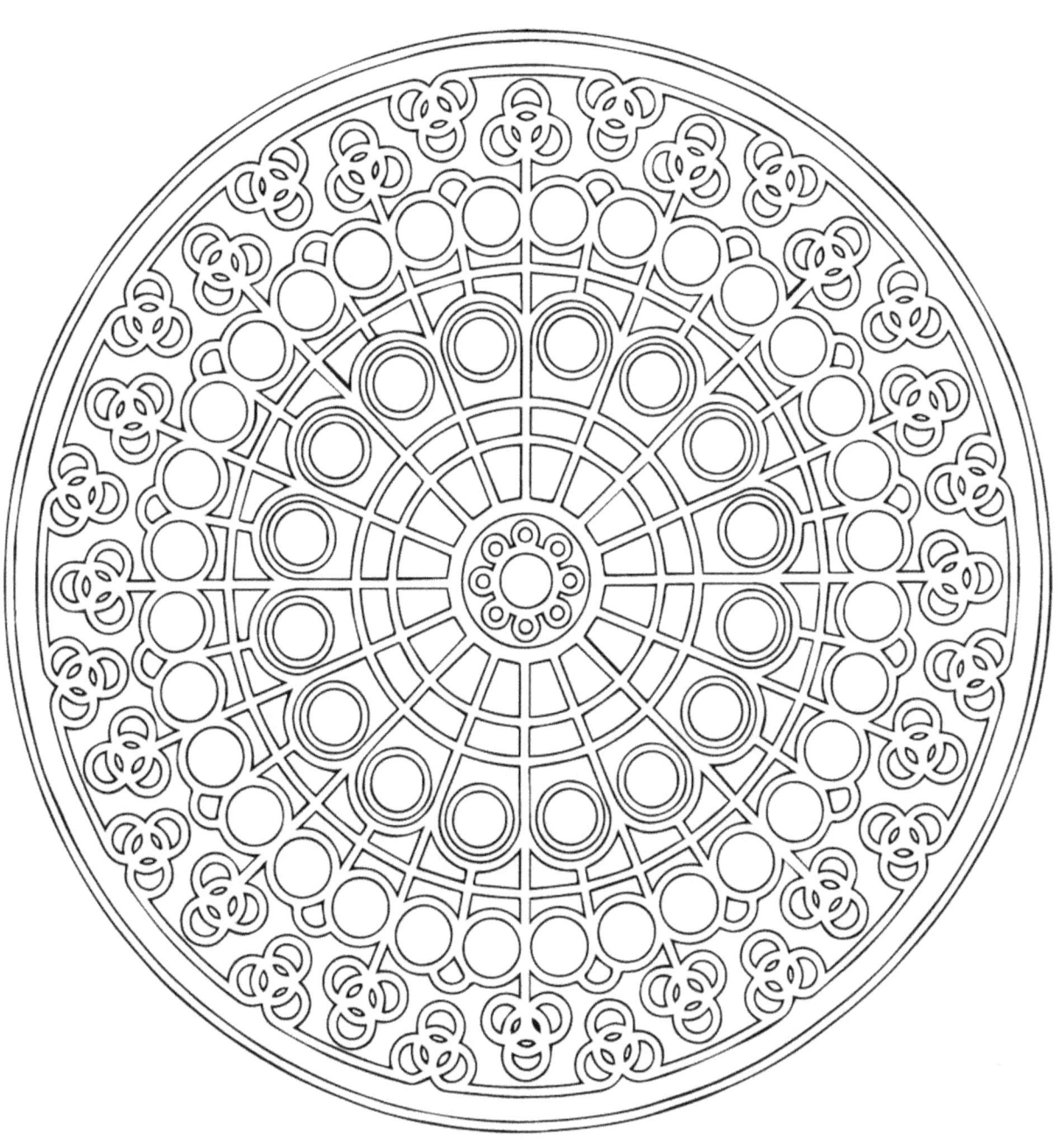

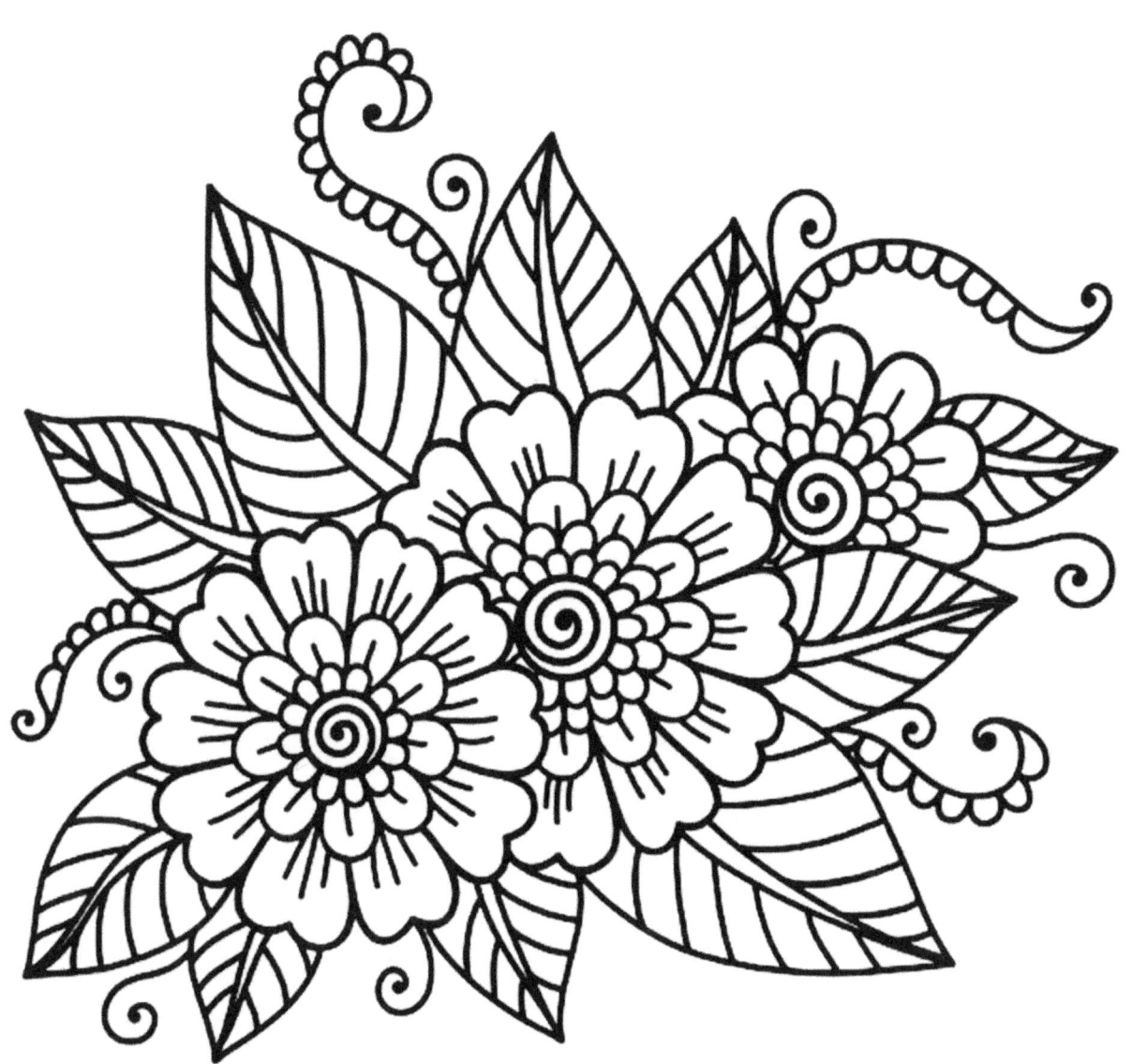

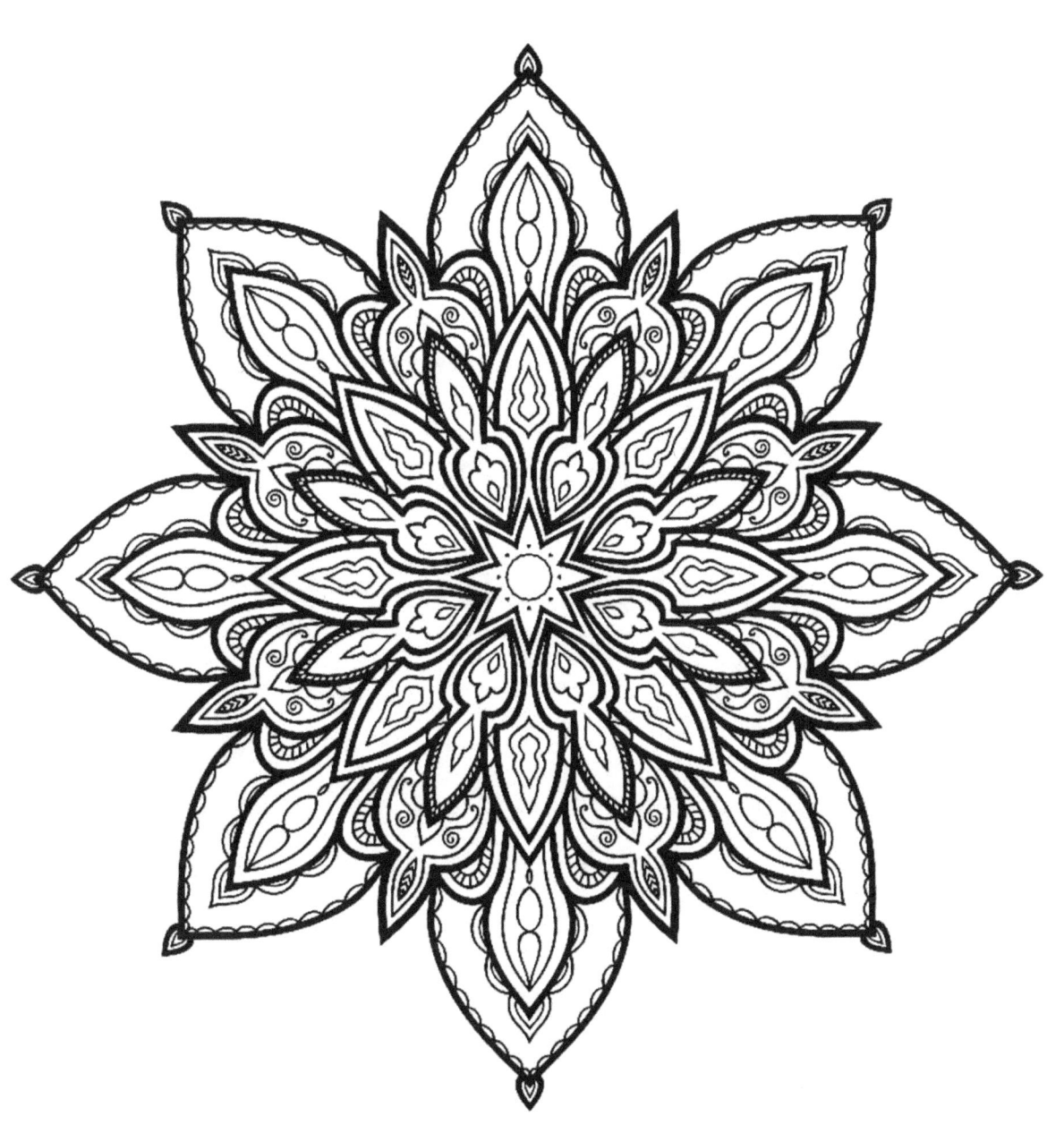

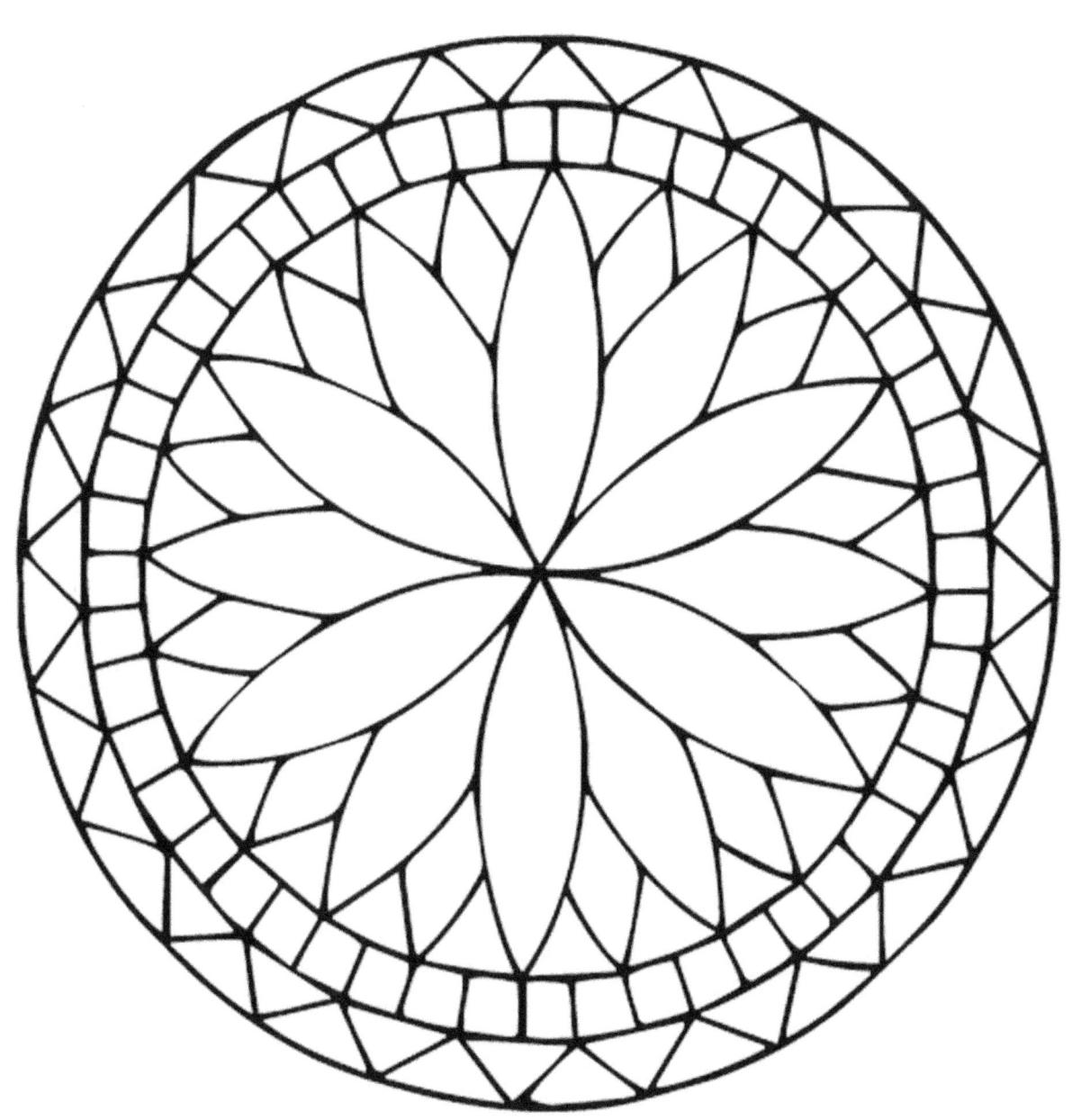

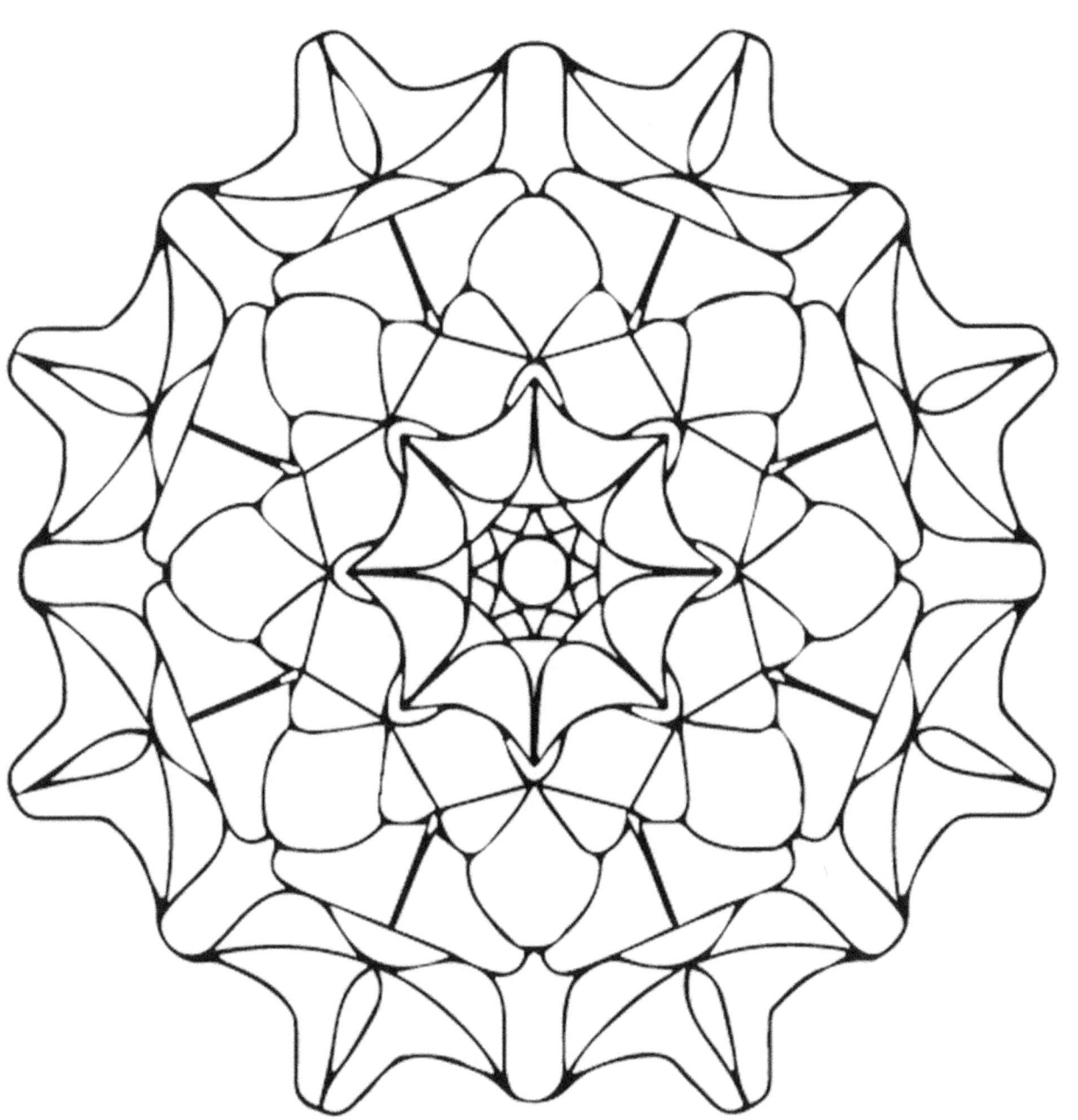

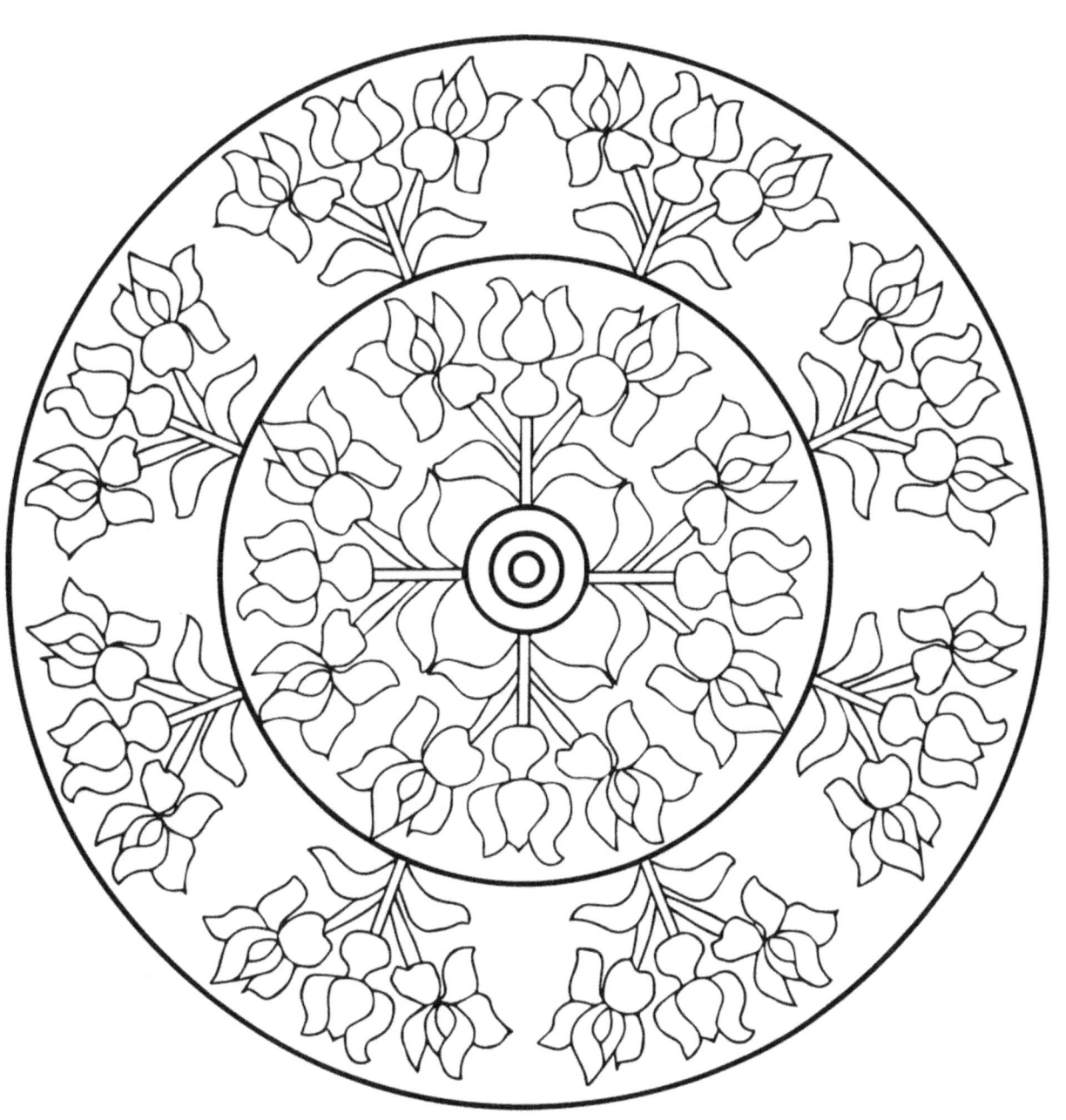

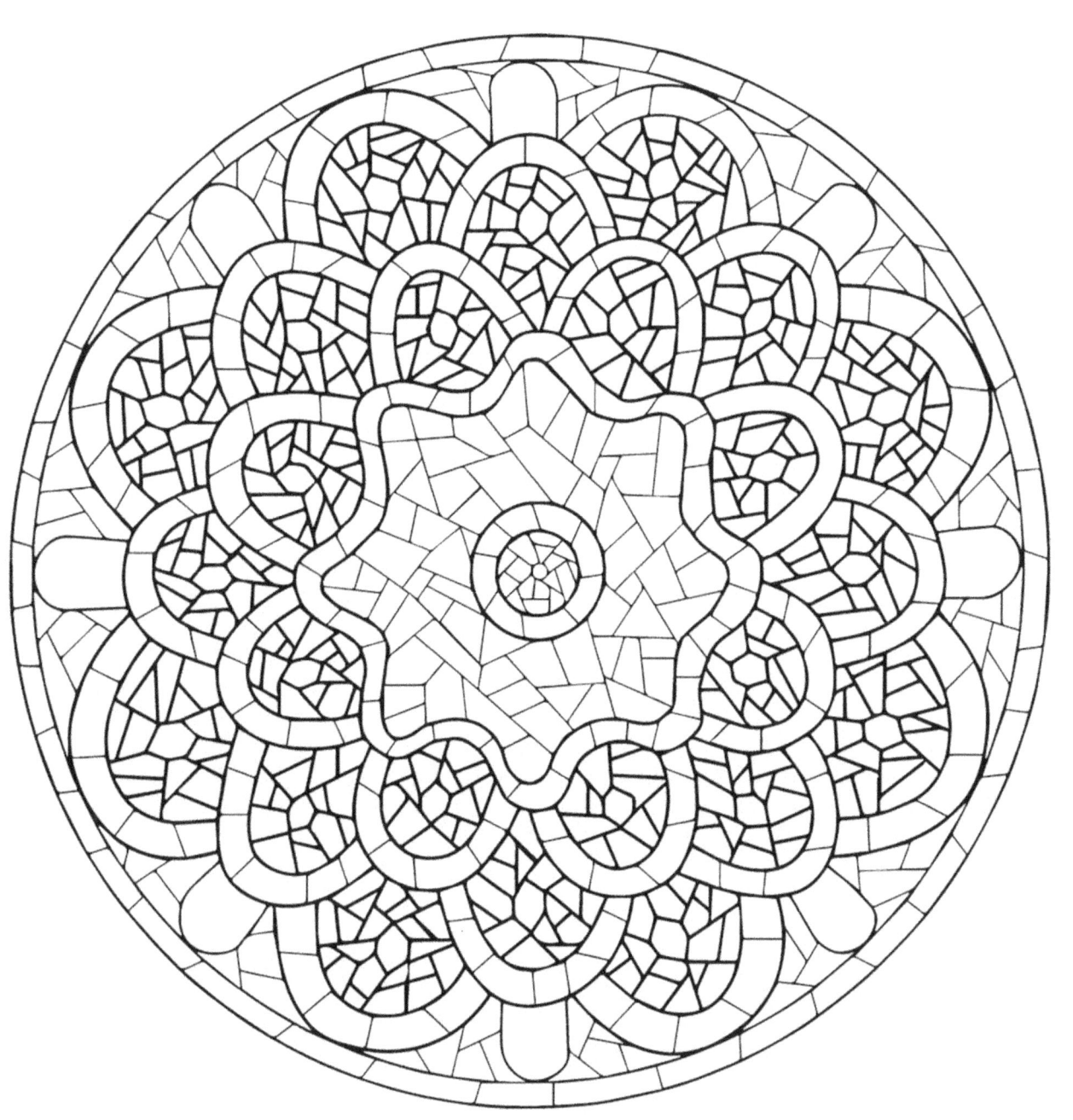

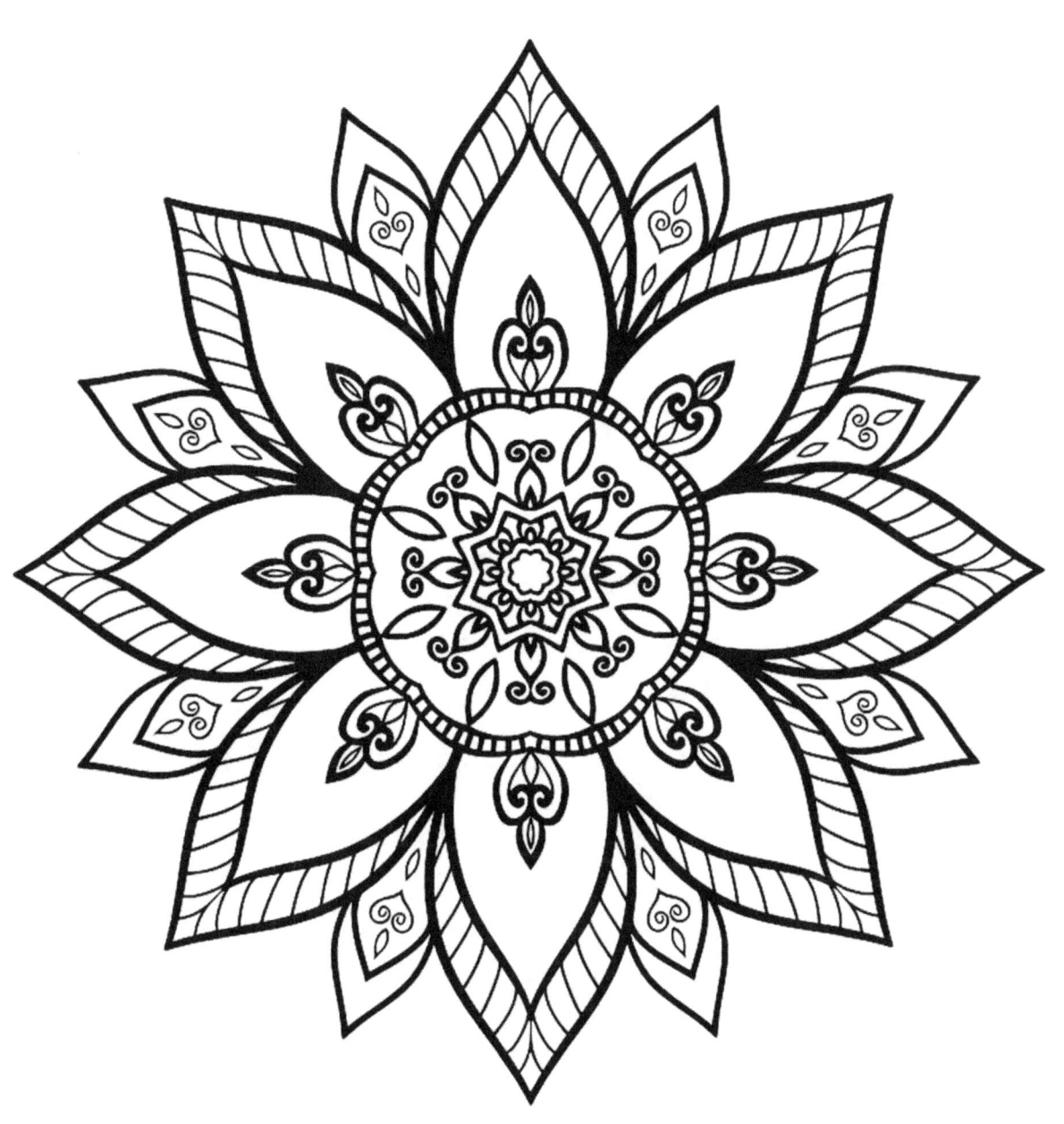

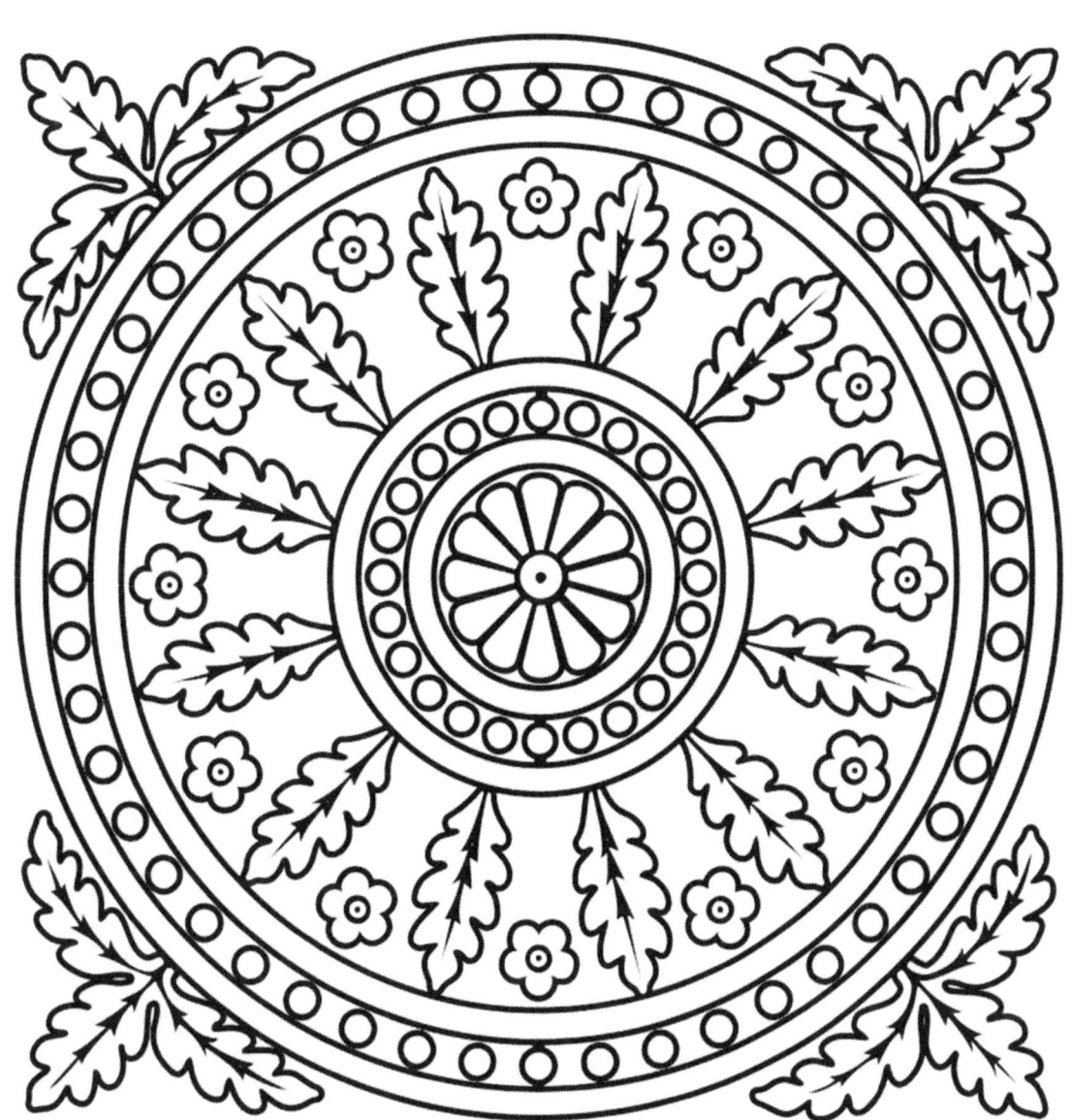

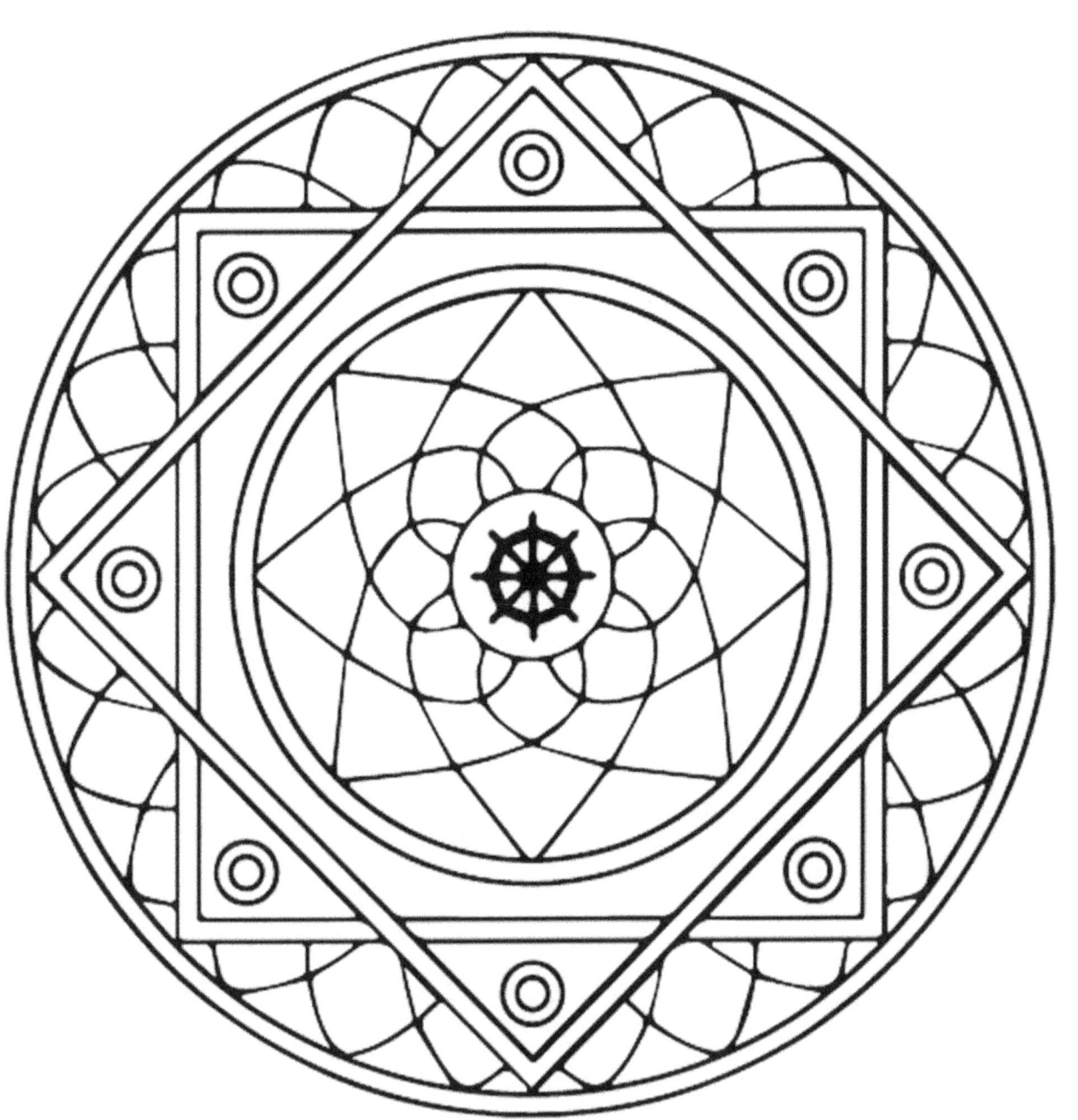

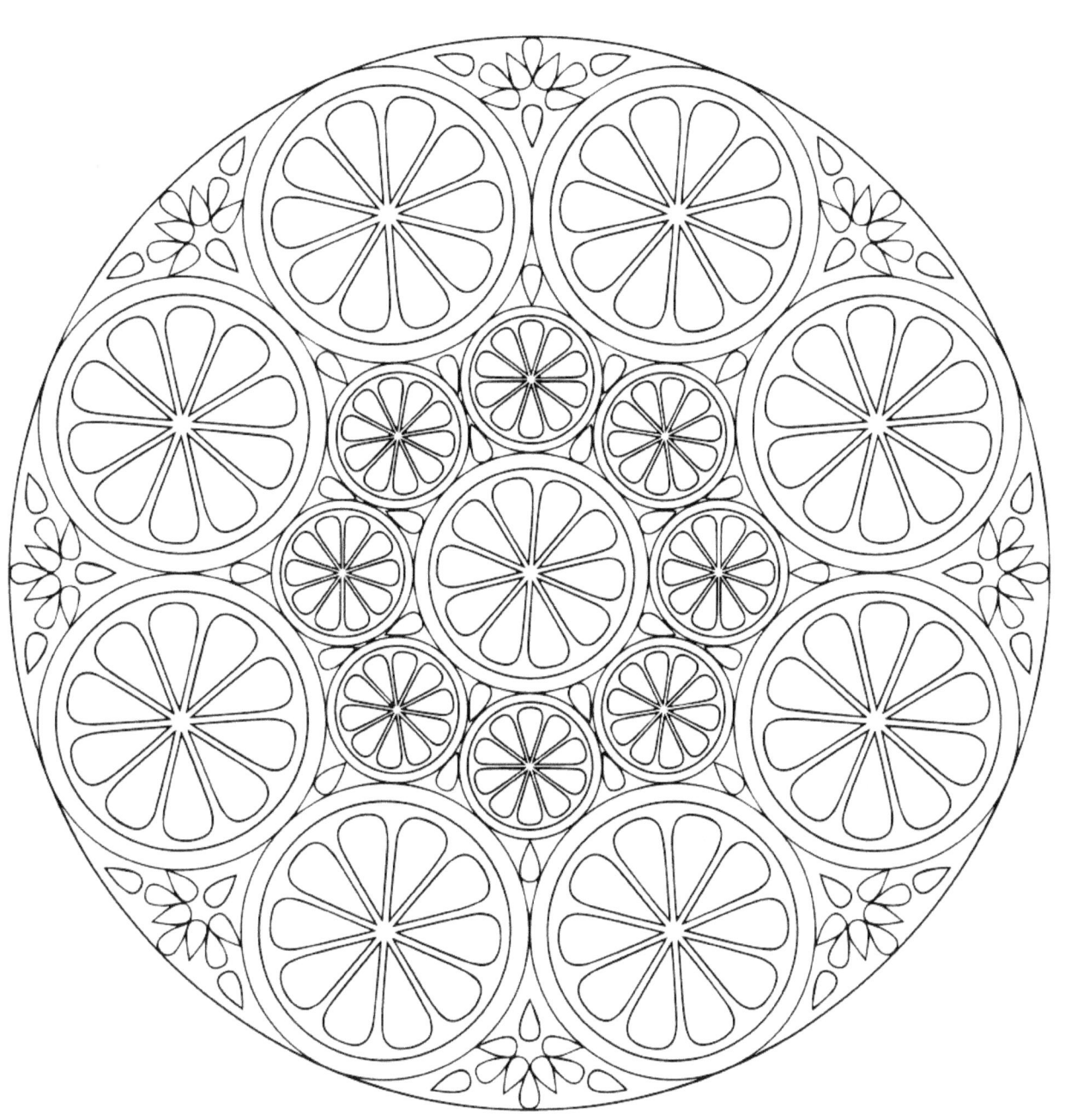

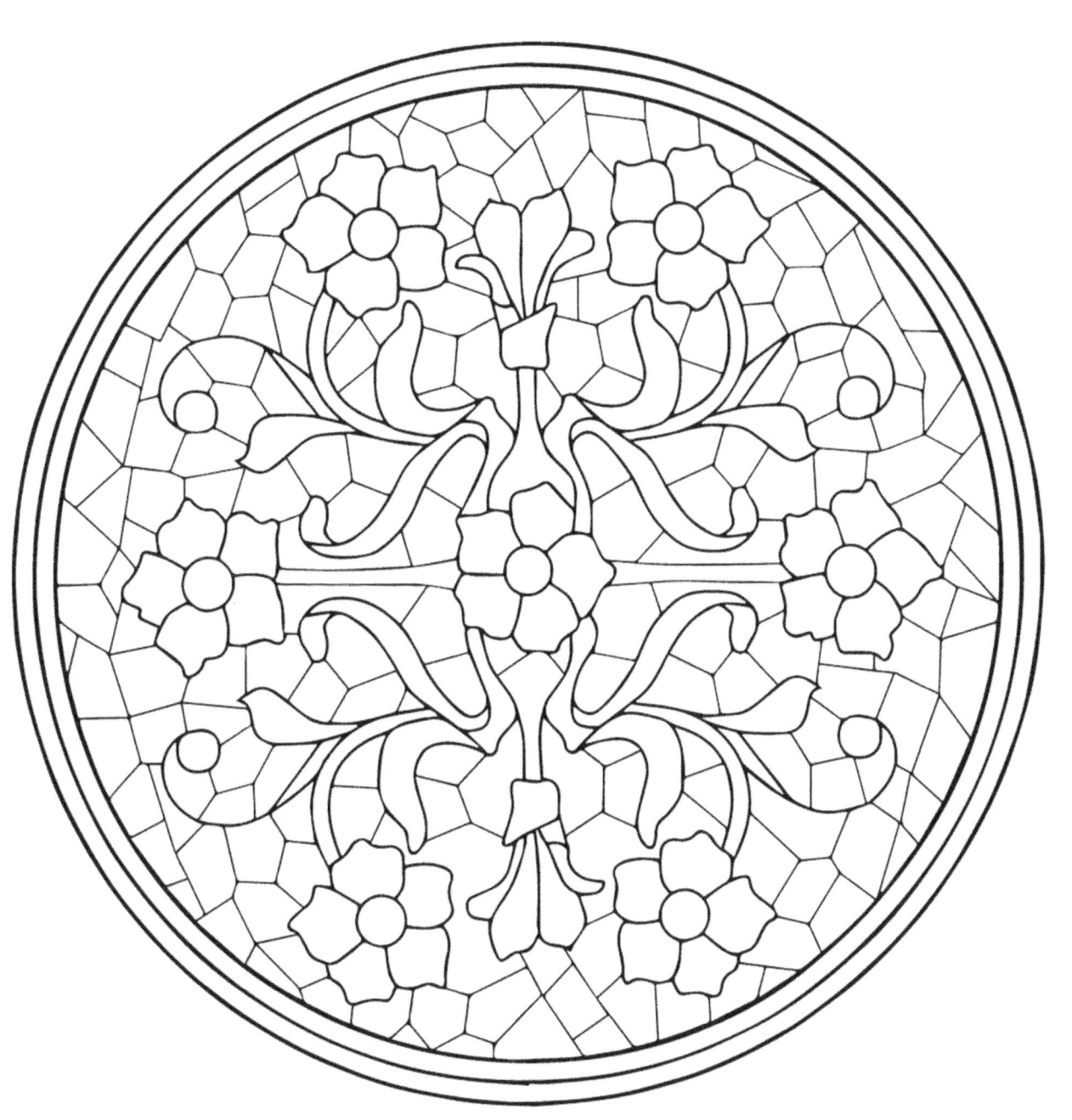

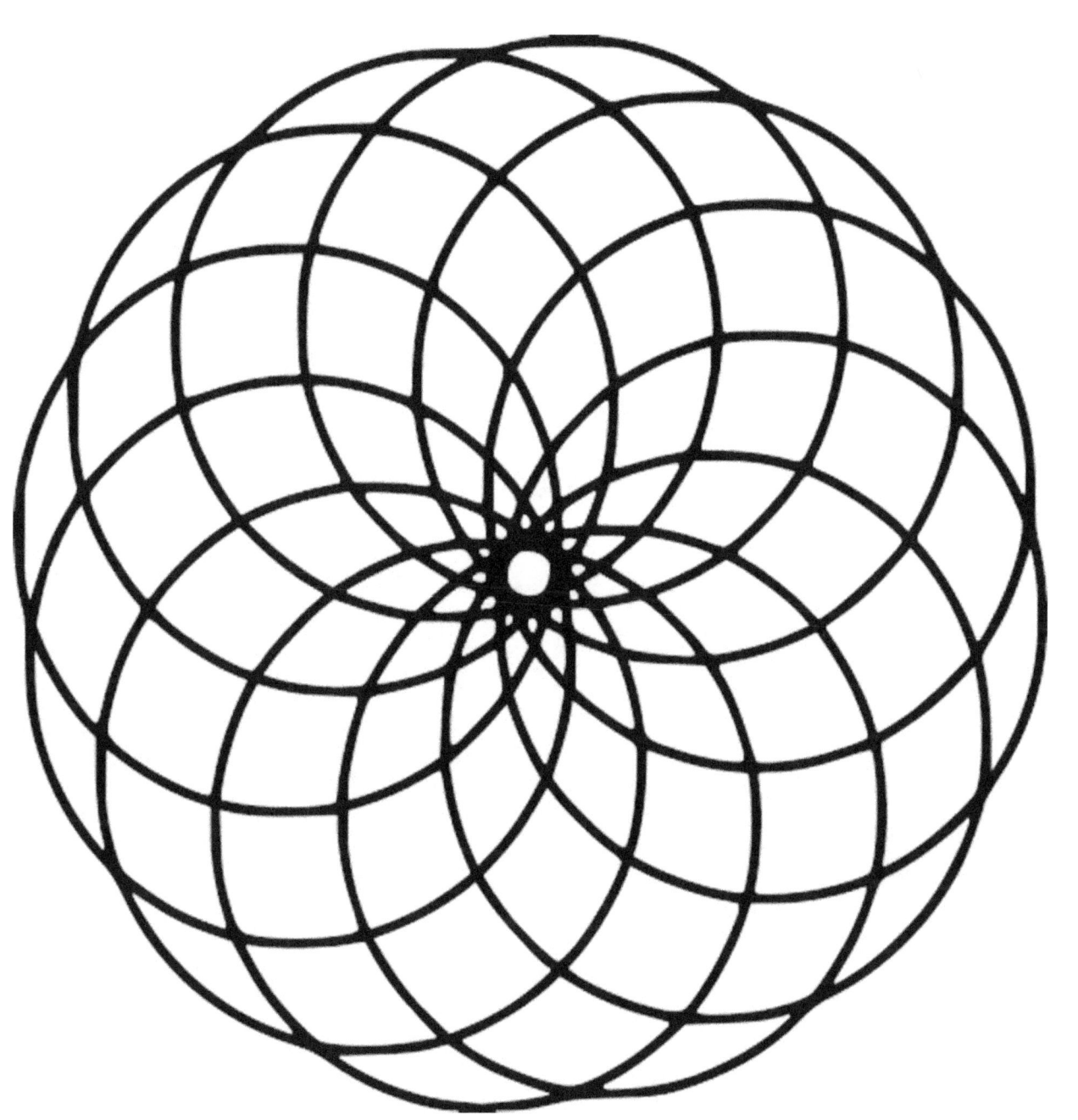

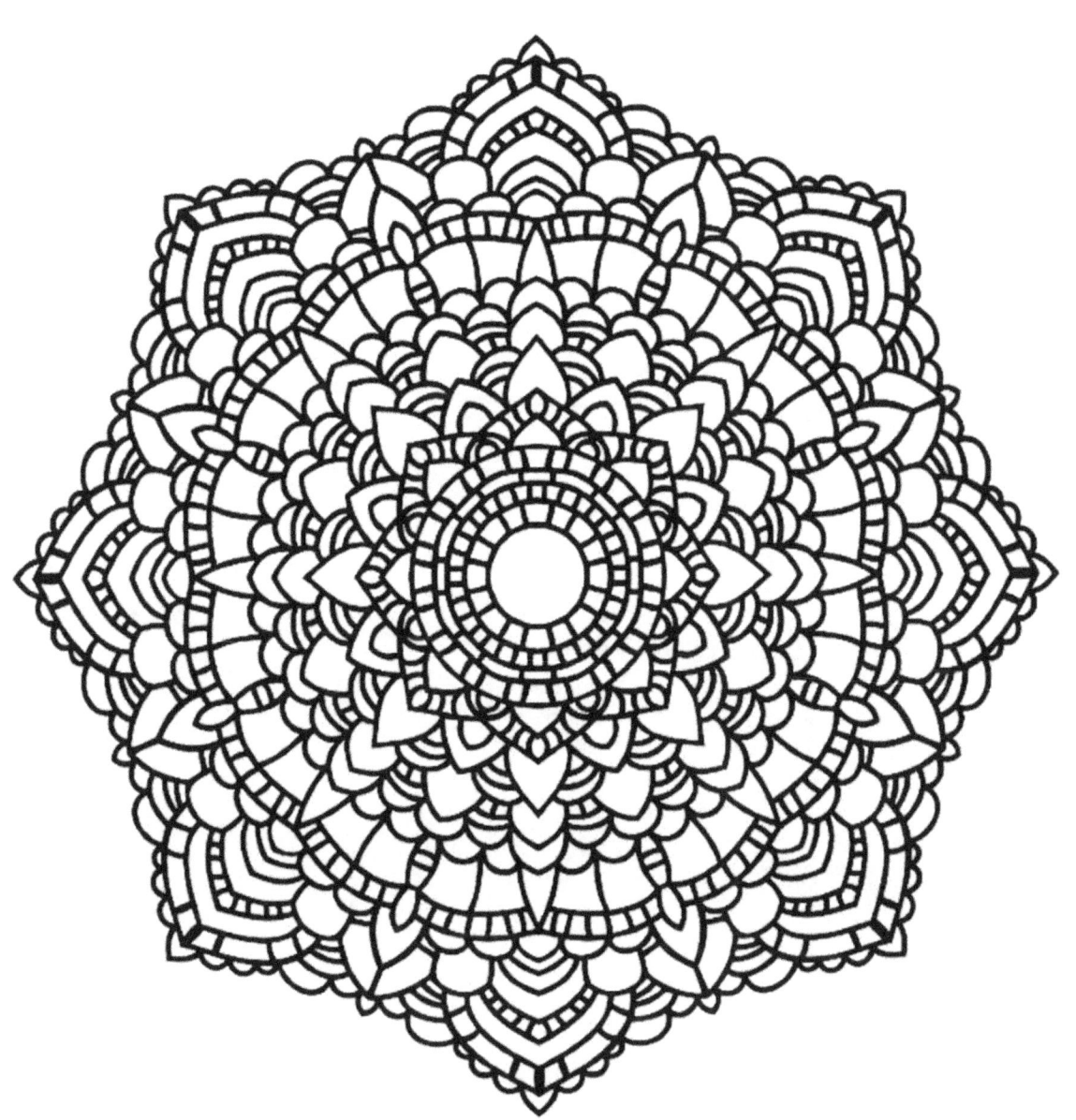

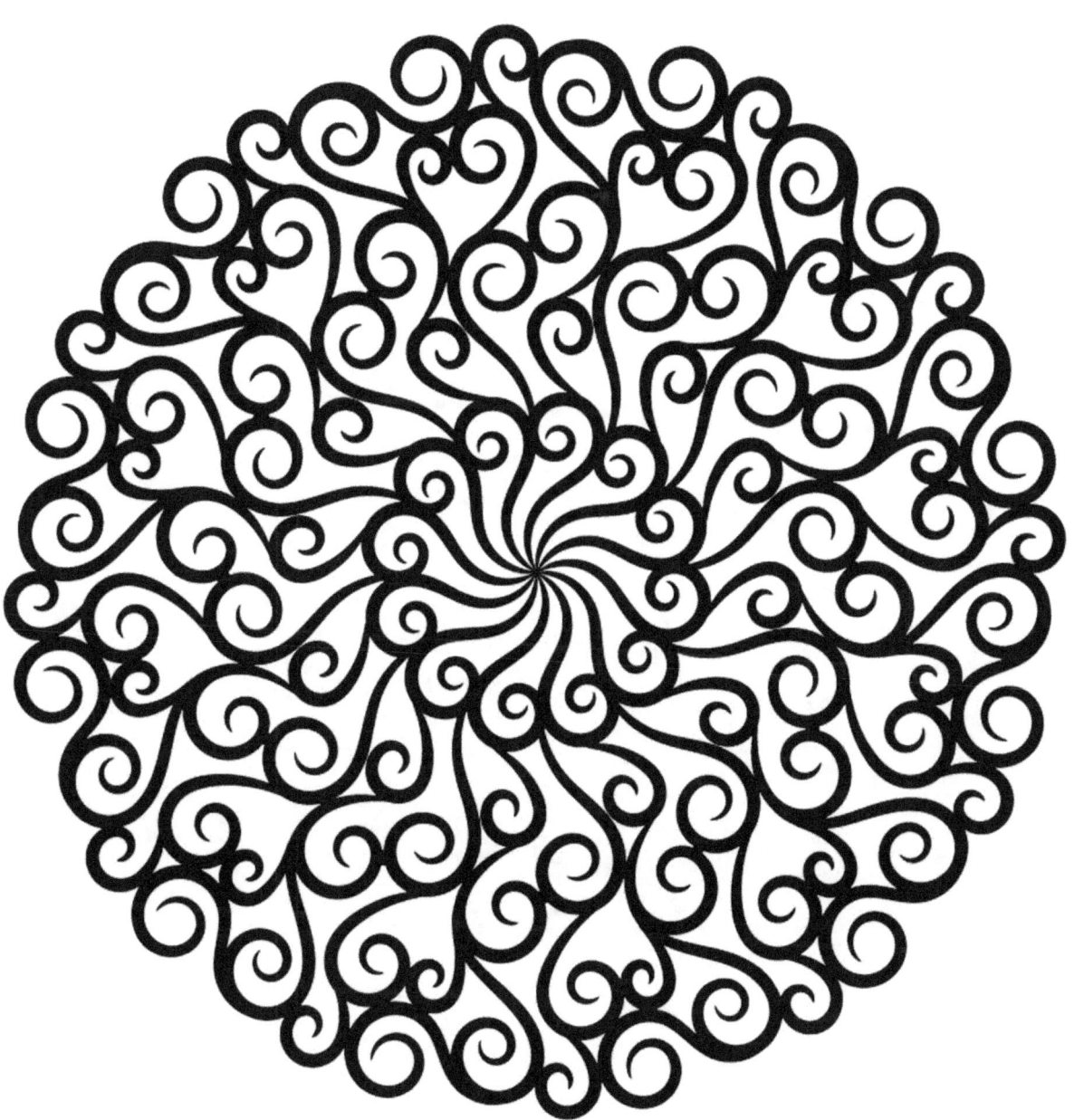

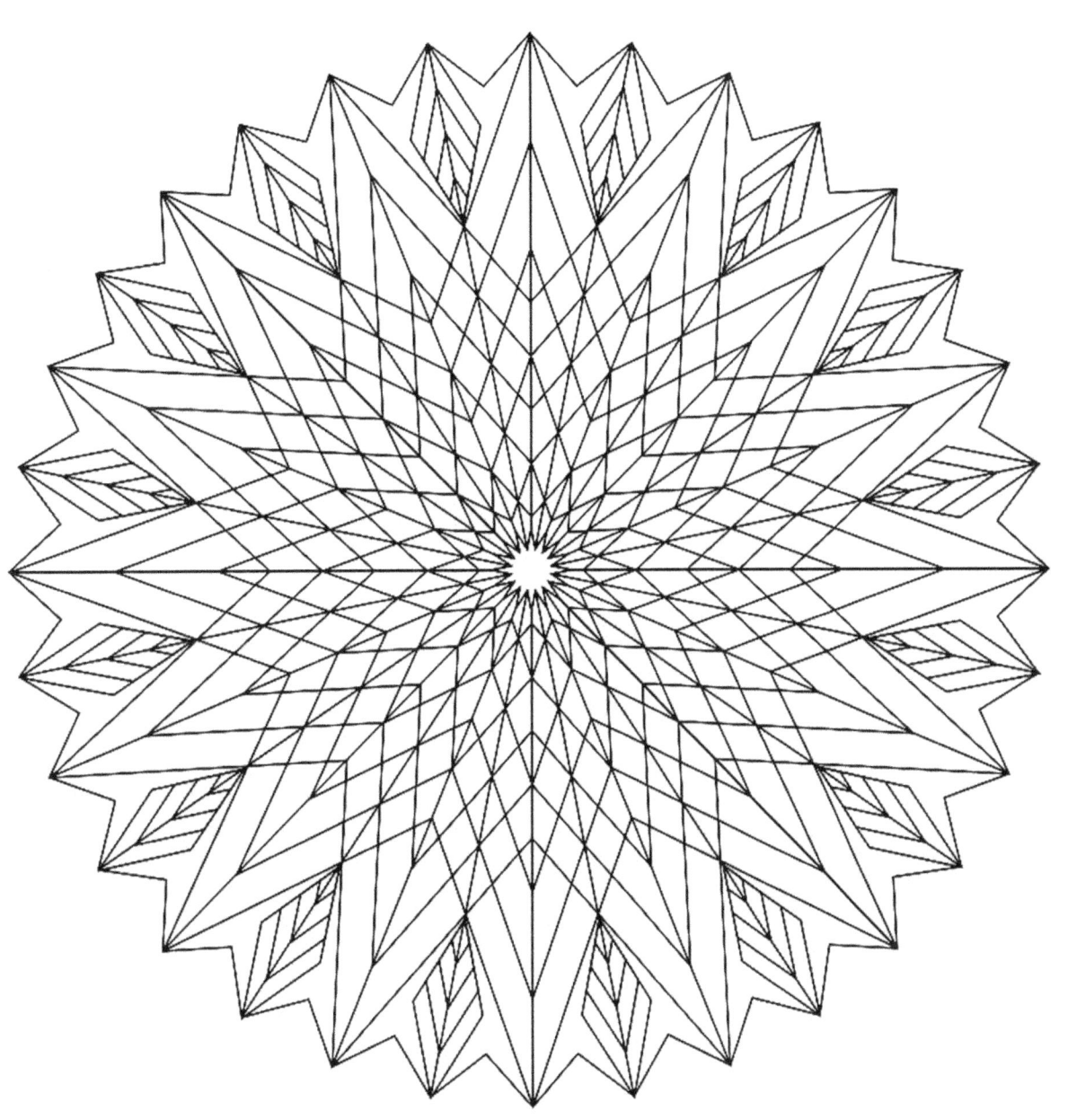

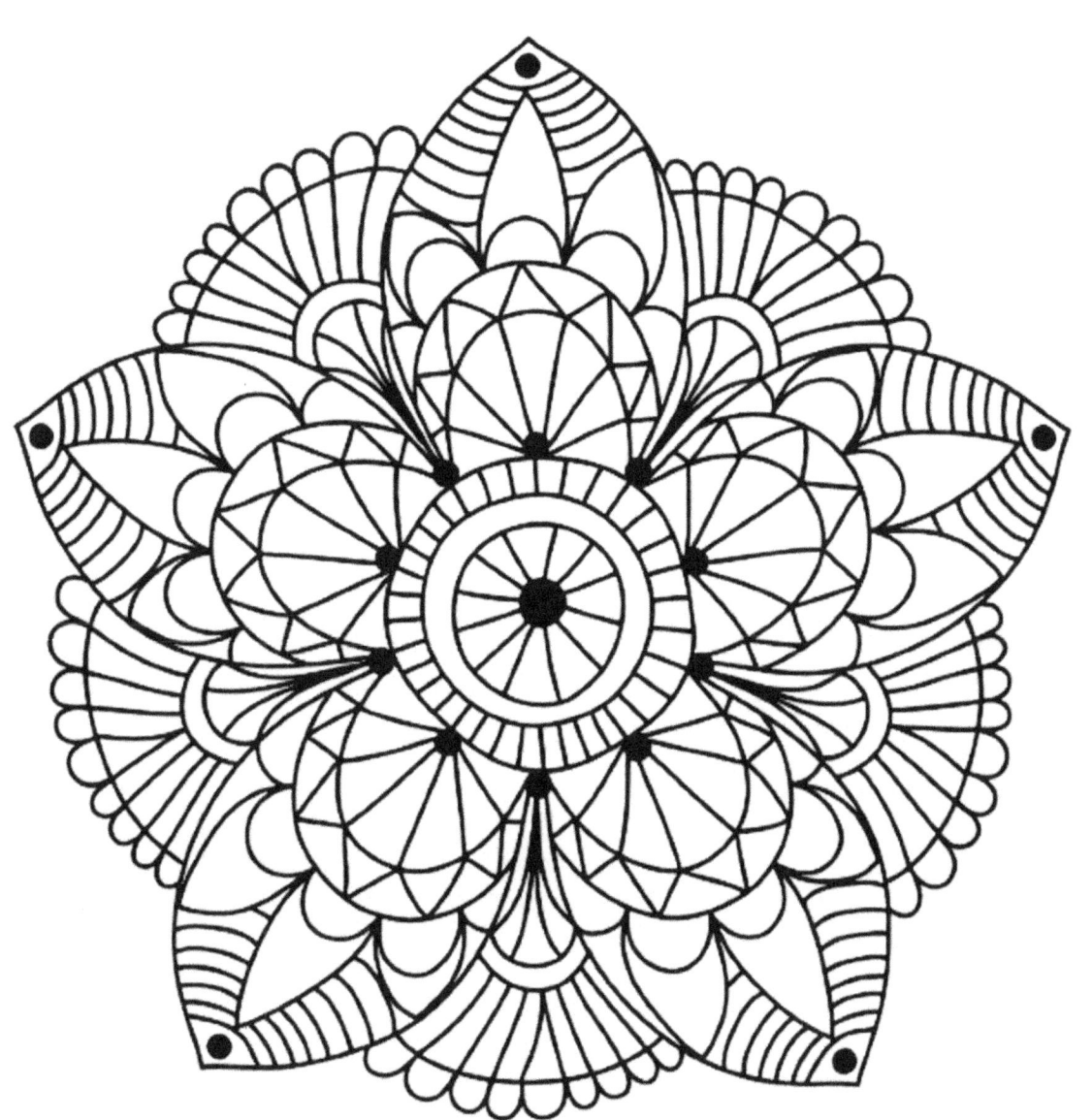

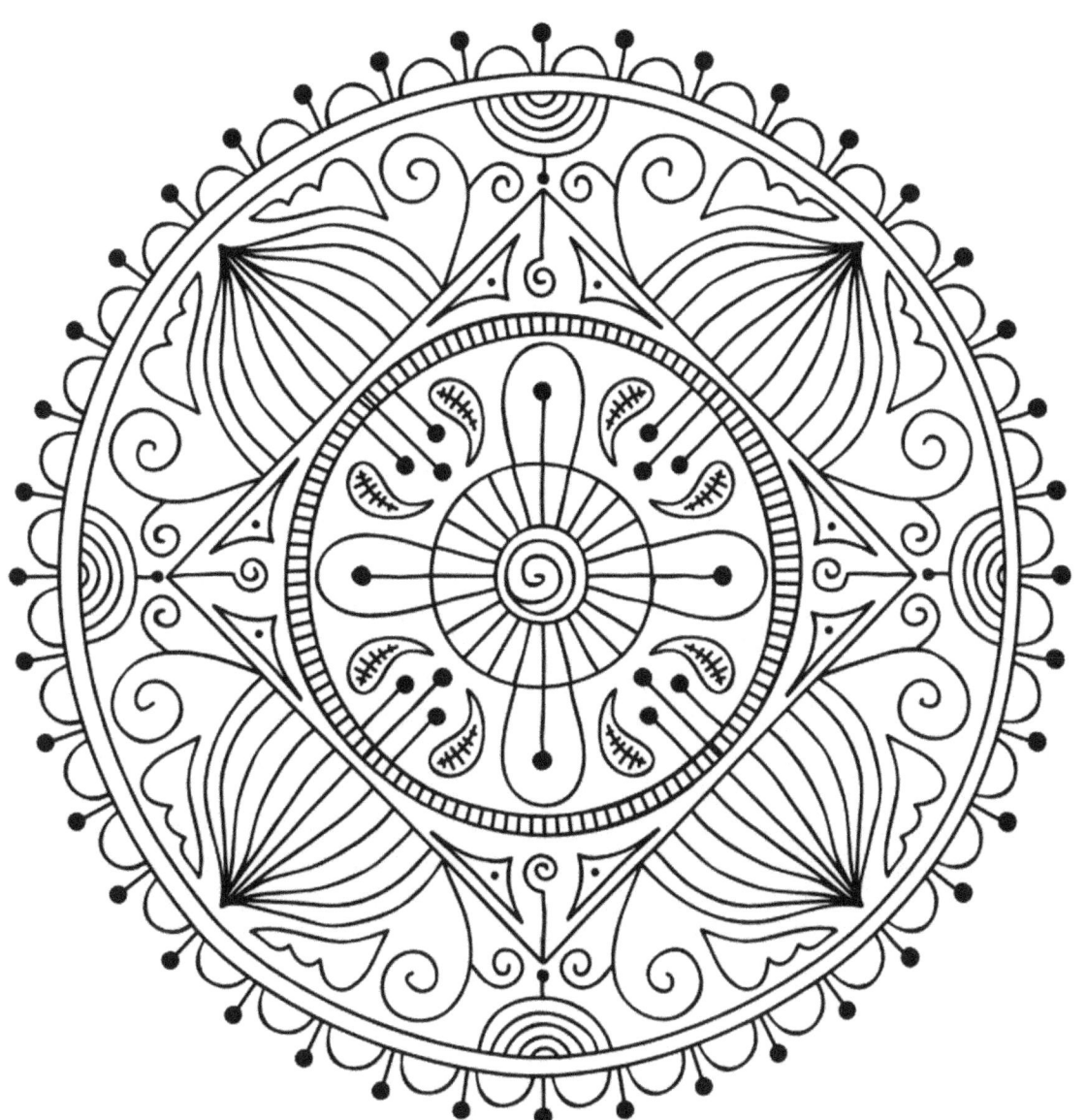

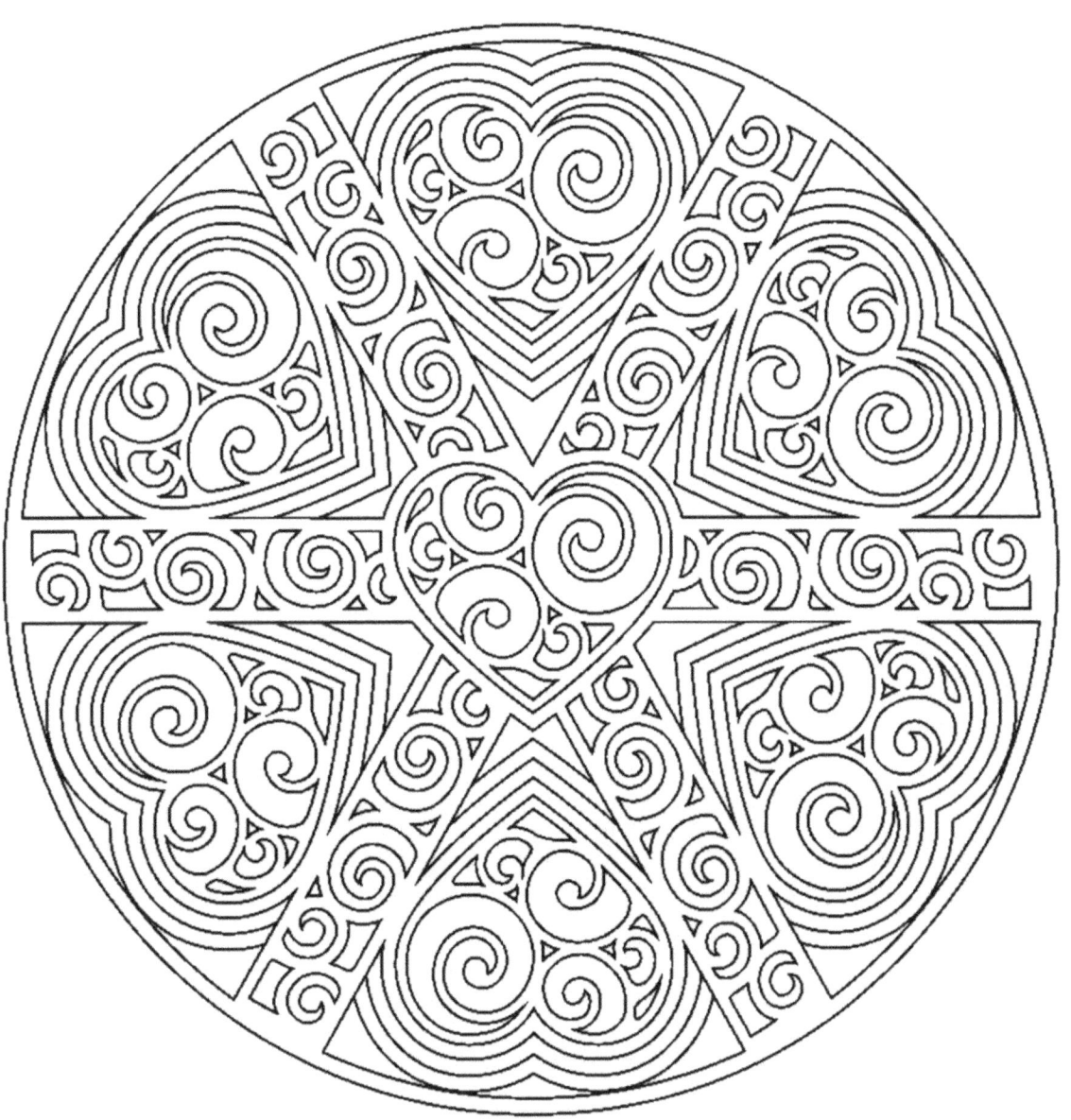

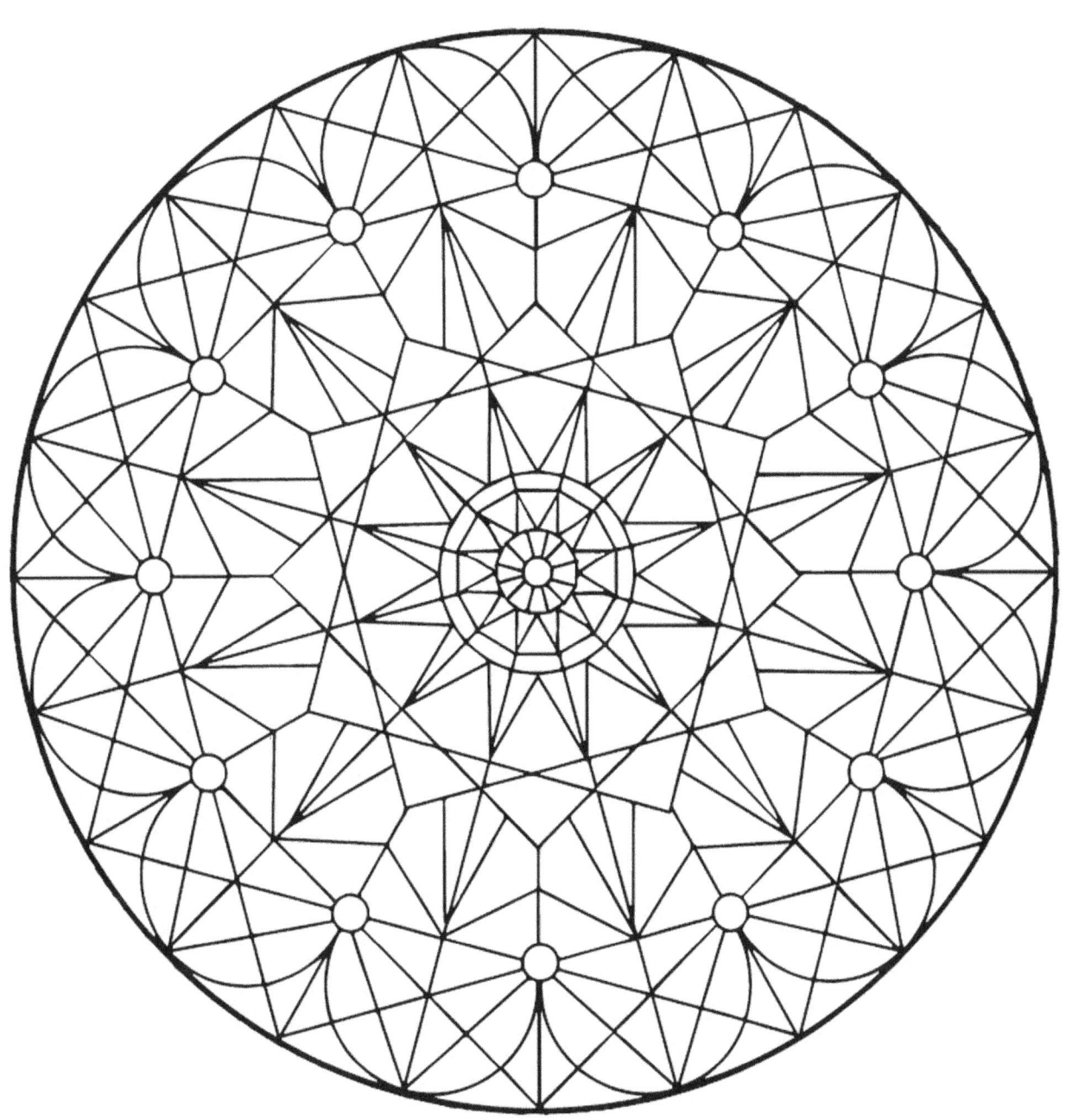

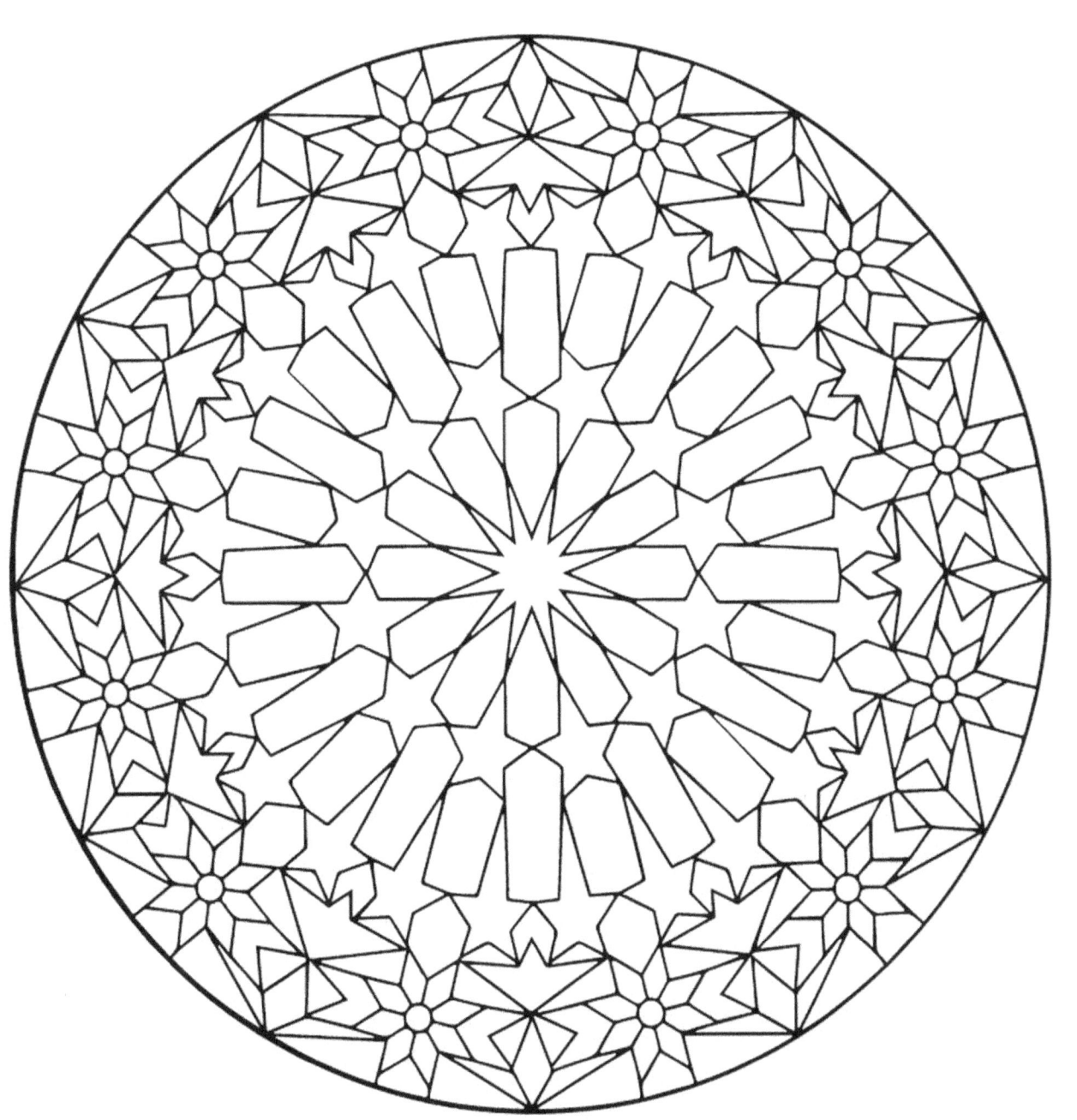

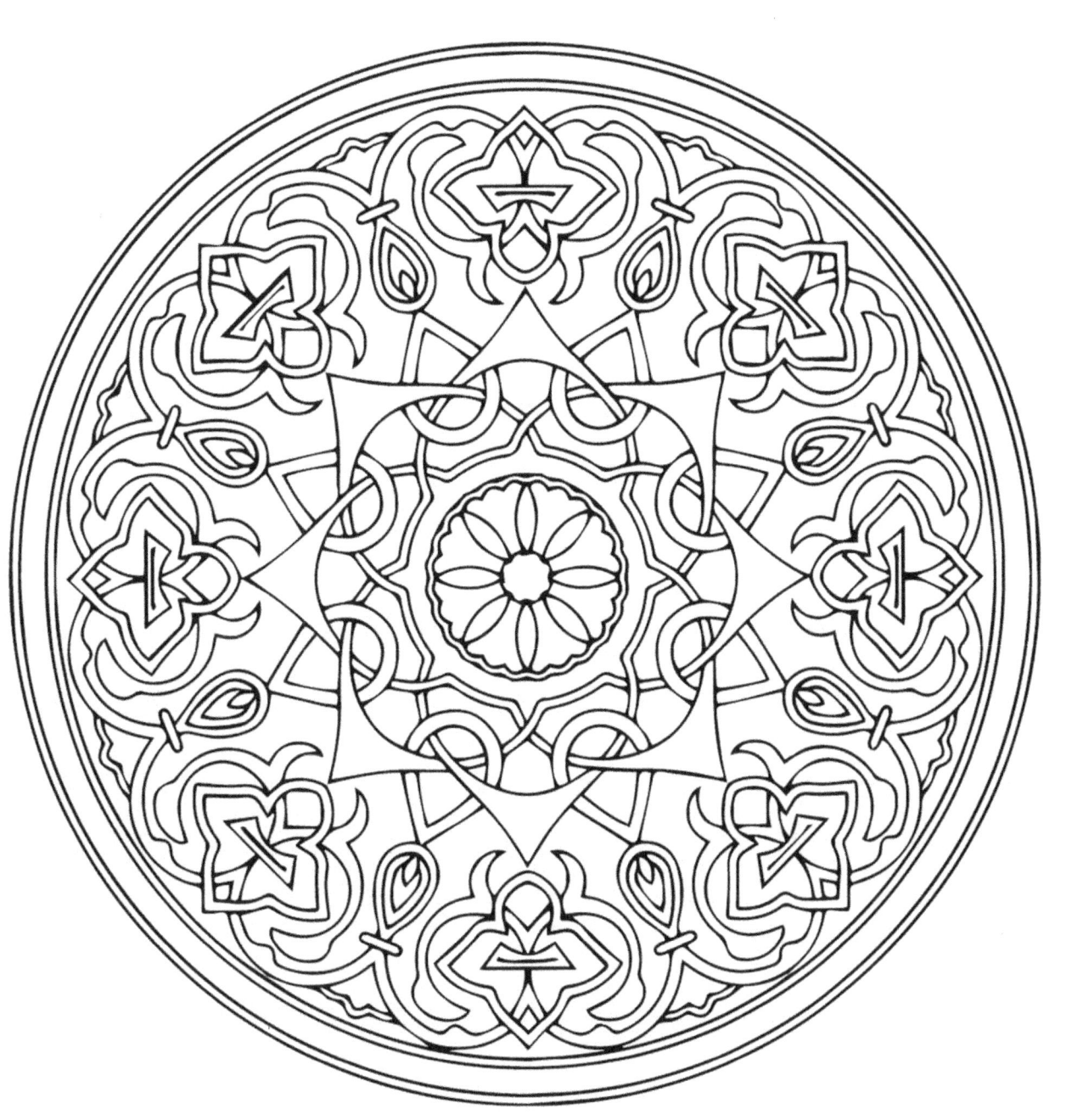

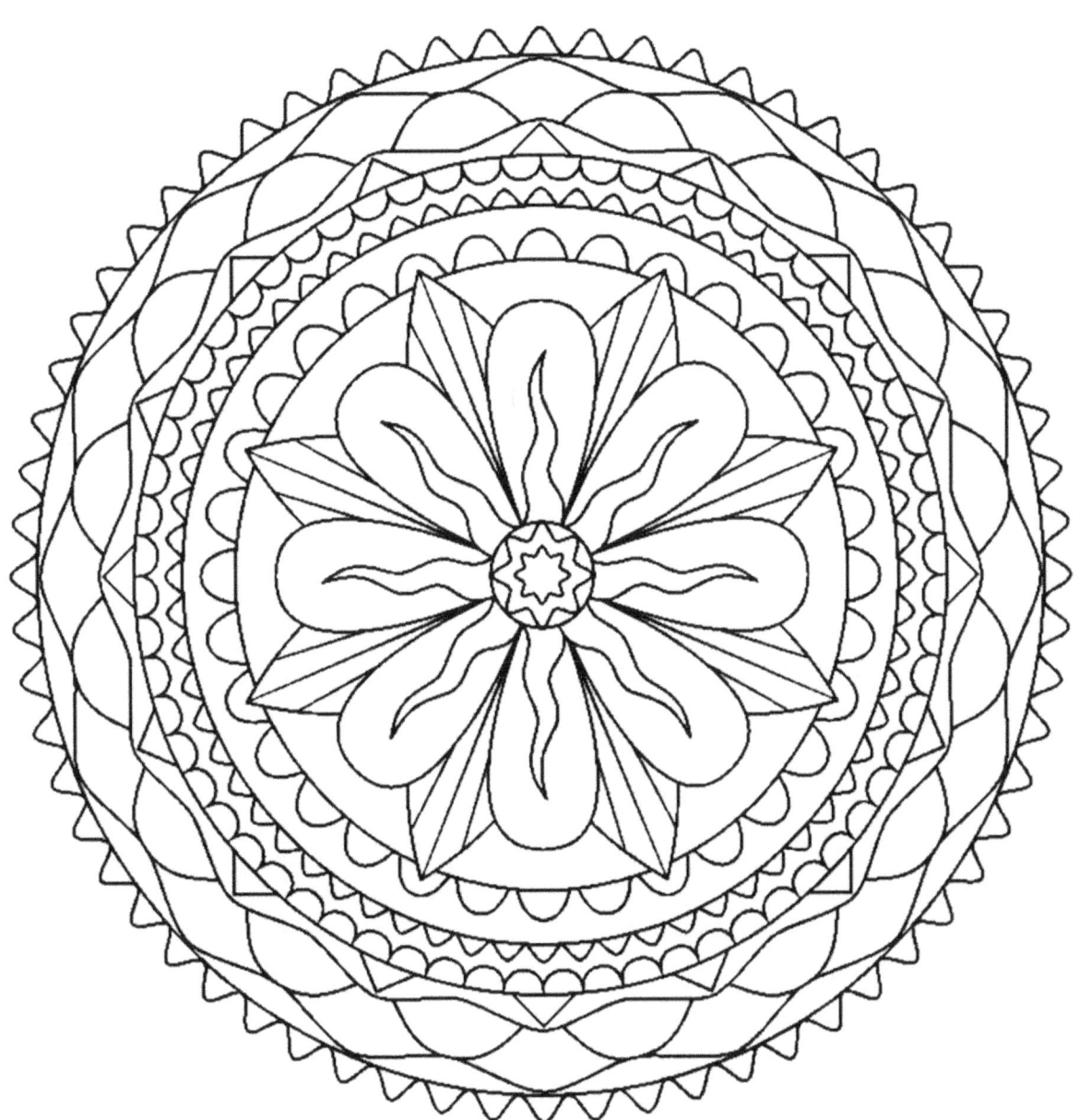

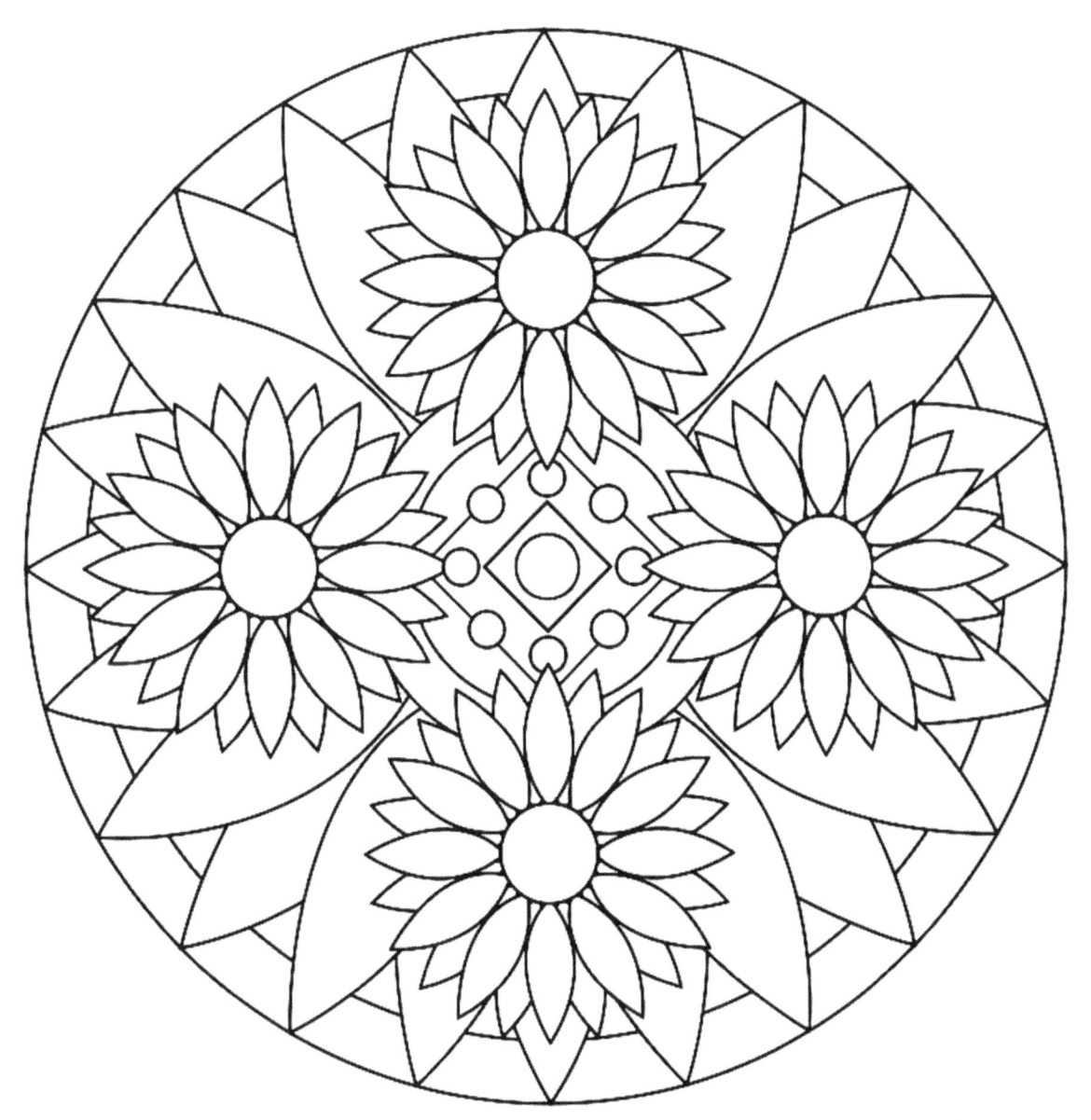

Thank you so much again for buying this book! I hope you enjoyed colouring my book. Now I'd like ask for a *small* favor. Could you please take a minute or two and leave a review for this book Amazon. It'd be greatly appreciated! And I truly value your opinion and thoughts and I will incorporate them into my next book, which is already underway.

www.ingramcontent.com/pod-product-compliance
Lightning Source LLC
Chambersburg PA
CBHW080632190526
45169CB00009B/3365